AN UNCONVENTIONAL JOURNEY..... AN UNLIKELY CHOICE

Angela L. Walker Franklin, Ph.D.

Wishing you the best !

Take care !

WESTBOW°
PRESS
A DIVISION OF THOMAS NELSON
& ZONDERVAN

WestBow Press books may be ordered through booksellers or by contacting:

WestBow Press
A Division of Thomas Nelson & Zondervan
1663 Liberty Drive
Bloomington, IN 47403
www.westbowpress.com
1 (866) 928-1240

ISBN: 978-1-4908-5465-6 (sc)
ISBN: 978-1-4908-5464-9 (e)

Library of Congress Control Number: 2014917510

Printed in the United States of America.

WestBow Press rev. date: 10/30/2014

CONTENTS

Acknowledgements vii

Introduction ix

Small-Town Girl.... Small- Town Values 1

Education is the Way.. 7

Psychology as the Foundation and the Pathway 11

A Medical School...Who Knew?..15

Finding Purpose.. 19

The Unlikely Choice..25

Lessons Learned 29

Leadership Qualities..33

Closing...43

References/Citations 45

ACKNOWLEDGEMENTS

I dedicate this book to my parents, Leola and Hervey Wesley Walker, Jr. because they instilled in me the core values which built the foundation for many of the lessons learned in leadership. My husband, Thaddeus Wadsworth Franklin, Jr. has also been my sounding board and confidant as I encountered the many challenges along the way. My sons, Wesley, Grant, and Jordan have been sources of great pride and sometimes comic relief, often giving me the reason to press on to be a great role model for them. I have love for them all and greatly appreciate all of their support.

I have had several individuals who have supported me in this journey outside of family. Many were instructors who were encouraging and convincing, often reminding me that I had what it takes to be successful. There were faculty advisors in college and graduate school who also reminded me of the value of hard work, dedication, and discipline. As my opportunities grew, I began to gravitate toward mentors in higher education. Dr. Louis W. Sullivan, Dr. Tom Norris, Dr. Larry Large, and Dr. George Keller were all influential at different points along the way. Although now deceased, I give the greatest tribute to Dr. George Keller, a well-respected leader in higher education and professor of higher education studies at University of Pennsylvania. It was Dr. Keller who first told me I needed to step out of my comfort zone and reach to pursue higher dreams. He also was the one who encouraged me to pursue the American Council on Education Fellows program.

There have been several colleagues along the way who helped me to shape my twelve principles of leadership, often learning from a situation or encounter that affirmed a particular approach.

I give a special thank you to my Executive Assistant, Christina Henderson, who was one of the first people to read my first draft and to provide feedback. In addition, I thank Barbara Boose, Kendall Dillon, and Julie Probst from the Des Moines University Department of Marketing and Communication who provided editorial assistance and creative cover design ideas.

The creation of this document was cathartic and reflective for me. Hopefully there are things that you can learn from my journey that will help you along your own life-path.

INTRODUCTION

I have the distinct honor of serving as a president and CEO of a health sciences university. My journey to this role has had considerable twists and turns, full of challenge, intrigue and trepidation. My experiences along the way have shaped a style of leadership that has prevailed, albeit sometimes challenged, depending upon the circumstances. I must admit, I did not start out with any particular "style" of leadership but with some basic principles of how to treat people and how I would want to be treated. Following the Golden Rule was instilled in me as a child, and it has shaped the approach and style of leadership that I bring with me to every environment and encounter.

The Golden Rule typically refers to treating others the way one would want to be treated. It is often associated with religious teachings and is an ethical code or guiding principle that has informed humanitarian efforts. Perhaps this Golden Rule is reflected in the Bible in Luke 10:27 as Jesus states, "You shall love the Lord your God with all your heart and with all your soul and with all your strength and with all your mind and your neighbor as yourself."

There are several other versions of the Golden Rule that you can find in many religious and philosophical traditions. For purposes of this document, I plan to keep it simply stated, e.g., "treating others the way you would want to be treated."

The basis for sharing my lessons learned along my career journey is intentional in helping you to find comfort in yourself as well as striving for success in all that you do. There is no "perfect" style of leadership, but perhaps some of the lessons learned along the way for me can be enlightening and inspirational to you along your own journey. I find that I have been on somewhat of an unconventional journey but yet, still, MY journey. I also have found that whereas I may have initially considered myself an unlikely choice for presidential leadership, there are lessons learned along the way that will cause me to delete the scripts of doubt that sometimes hold us all back.

I continue to grow and learn more about myself as I journey along the way, and I also find that the lessons learned continue to expand as time goes on. So I continue to be a work in progress, and that is just fine. This is my unconventional journey... with a presumption of being an unlikely choice for leadership.

SMALL-TOWN GIRL....
SMALL- TOWN VALUES

I was born in Greenwood, South Carolina, at Brewer Hospital. It no longer exists as it was the hospital for "colored" people. South Carolina in the '60s was not that progressive in terms of race relations, and there clearly were remnants of the Jim Crow South.

I have very distinct memories from my childhood of going to our local physician and having to sit on the "colored" side of the waiting room. I also recall never seeing a movie in my hometown because the theatre had seating for "colored" in the balcony. My parents were vehemently opposed to going to such places if we could not otherwise be treated like everyone else. That posture also explained why we only frequented certain places of business in town, given that my parents had a strong conviction of fairness and equality. Luckily, we often went outside of my hometown for better treatment.

I was fortunate to have educated and prosperous parents. Lucky, too, perhaps, that I was born into a household with resources that many did not have. Hervey Wesley Walker, Jr., my father, a mortician, owned the only funeral home for African Americans in my hometown. He, a son of an AME (African American Episcopal) minister, had the opportunity to go to college, then on to medical school at Meharry

1

Medical College in Nashville, Tennessee. Yet duty called to help out the family business, and he left medical school after one year and traveled to New York City to enroll in embalming school instead. He returned to McCormick, South Carolina after completing his training to work in the family business and continues to run Walker's Funeral Home now over 60 years later. He met Leola Marian Grant, my mother, also a native of McCormick, South Carolina there. She, a graduate of Paine College (a historically black college/university) in Augusta, Georgia, had completed her bachelor's degree in education with teacher certification and had returned as an elementary school teacher in McCormick. There, they established their longstanding roles in the community as engaged civic leaders and raised two daughters. My sister, Maria, came first, and three years later I arrived.

McCormick, South Carolina, clearly is a small town. Over the years, it has changed very little and continues to remain a small, rural community to this day. That is where I began, where I learned the importance of relationships and people, and where people, today, still would call me "one of Junior Walker's girls"!

There truly is something to say about small-town values. First, in a small town you come to value relationships and people in a way that causes you to think first of others sometimes before yourself. I often heard my father, as a local businessman, talk about the value of treating people with respect because he served the public. Growing up with a father businessman and a mother educator, also taught me the value of following the Golden Rule; treating others as you would want to be treated. Echoing in my head even to this day is the phrase my father often used about his business of serving the public: "It is my livelihood!"

In a small town, there is also a sense of looking out for each other and there was really no way to hide because everyone knew who you were. We were somewhat under a microscope, and everyone in town knew who we were. There were clear expectations set for how we interacted with others.

On the other hand, it sometimes appeared as if we were more concerned about what others would think than about what may be best for us. For instance, I clearly remember some conversations my parents had about a piece of property in town with a very nice two-story home. We could have afforded it, but my father was too concerned about the image and the impression people would have about us living in a home that would set us apart from the average. So we continued to live in a very modest home next door to the funeral home. That is my family home, and my parents continue to reside there today.

Being one of Junior Walker's girls meant we essentially grew up in a fish bowl. There was always a concern about treating people right because my father's business served the public. And, unfortunately, business was "good" when there was a death in a family. There was an intriguing dynamic that caused people to both "fear" the Walkers and respect us all at the same time. At a time of need, there was an expectation of compassion, sincerity and empathy. Yet there was also the fear of death and dying, and I often had to hear the jokes that scary things would happen to you if you came into the funeral home.

My job once I learned to play the piano well enough to be the church pianist was to go to all the funerals and provide music, especially in those small rural churches that often did not have their own pianist. I drove the hearse sometimes at the beginning of the processionals and occasionally drove the family limousines. I had just as much fun, however, driving the grave diggers around in the truck, because I could be finished sooner with my duties if I did not have to drive the family car and take them back to their home.

What I remember most about those days, which lasted through high school for me, was the sense of community, respect and being of service to those in need. I was often frustrated that it meant we could rarely leave town on vacation because someone needed to be on-call 24-7-365. My father rarely left town and, if he did, it was only for a quick trip, sometimes racing to get back if there was a call about another death. As the only embalmer, even to this day, it meant he could not be too far away in the event of another death.

I often wondered why anyone would want to live this way. The funeral home essentially became a "ball and chain", and there were sometimes jokes that morticians were no more than "buzzards", hovering around dead people, waiting to land and scoop them up. It was not a "happy" business to be in and it was always very sad and sorrowful. Frankly, neither I nor my sister ever imagined continuing to work in the family business. Instead we were determined to leave this little town to pursue much more exciting, interesting and fun careers. Little did we know we would both land in the health professions, still destined to help people and to be of service.

McCormick, South Carolina, in the '60s/'70s was still a very segregated existence. There was very little mixing of the races and interracial marriage was even against the law. I started elementary school at Mims Elementary School, the black school in town where my mother taught 6th grade English. However, closer to me in my neighborhood was McCormick Elementary School, which was for whites only. As a little kid growing up in the segregated South, I never imagined a world of integrated schools because it simply was not expected. Frankly, it was a foreign concept. In spite of that, I was blessed to be raised by parents who were staunch supporters of the civil rights movement and equality. There was an expectation for high academic achievement and a real belief that regardless of where we were or what school we attended, we would be successful.

I remember the debate by my parents of whether to send me and my sister away for boarding school to be able to get a more rigorous education. They had the resources but they also were concerned about community backlash. As community leaders, my parents felt to remove us from the community would send a message that we thought we were "better than others." So, with my mother teaching in the local school district, they decided it would be best if her children remained in that same local school district. There was a way however, to give us the extra academic enrichment that she felt we needed by sending us away during the summers for additional educational experiences. We were expected to achieve, and the foundation for success was laid.

The lessons learned from this small-town existence were forever ingrained in me. They were as follows: 1) treat people with respect, 2) live conservatively with little flash and fanfare, 3) expect and demand to be treated equally, 4) strive for success and aspire to achieve at a level much higher than anyone's expectations, and 5) remember the Golden Rule.

EDUCATION IS THE WAY

There was no question that educational achievement was a core value of the Walker family. My sister paved the way and I followed, often receiving straight A's and winning numerous awards each year. We were also both accomplished musicians; piano and flute for me, and piano and clarinet for her.

In the late '60s however, the town of McCormick was still struggling with the national mandates for integration. The *Brown vs Board of Education* case in 1954 was to end school segregation. This ruling was to give black children in the South access to equal education, but several years later, many southern states refused to enforce school desegregation. Actually, it was not until 1970 that McCormick County finally integrated the public schools.

My parents had been approached with the idea of having my sister and me to be the first to integrate McCormick Elementary School. Although initially concerned about the difficulty we may face, they decided to move forward and enroll us there in 1969. So I began my 4th grade year as the only black student in my class. My sister, in 7th grade, was one of two black students.

I have vivid memories of being the only person of color in my 4th grade class. The experience of moving from the all-black school to the all-white school was a bit uncomfortable initially, but, I quickly adjusted. I recall it being very important for my parents, however, to make sure we continued to be straight A students. It was as if there was a need to validate to the public that we were actually "smart" and our grades were not just given because of who we were.

I have fun memories from that year as I developed very good friendships with several of my classmates. However, I did not realize how much of an experiment this really was for the small town of McCormick. I remember going for a play date at one of my friends' house and it was just as much fun as any other play date. However, it was the first time I was in the home of a white family. Little did I know there was real concern by some of their neighbors about the fact that I was there. Frankly, black and white children just did not go to each other's homes to play in my hometown.

The greater insult to me, however, came a year later when I advanced to the 5th grade. By then, McCormick had integrated the schools, but most of my friends from the white elementary school were removed from the public school system in protest of integration and their parents enrolled them in private schools. Many of these schools were several miles away. Thus, the beginning of "white flight." So my best friend from 4th grade could no longer be my friend because she was removed from going to school with us. Sadly, I never interacted with her again.

I was not sure what to think during those times, but it gave me reason to question equality and whether or not it was possible to have good relationships with other races. I seemed to have an easy time making friends regardless of race but frankly thought it was not welcomed. So you learn to adjust and remain distant even when opportunities are presented.

By the time I graduated from McCormick High School it was predominately black as white flight had worked. Although I was very comfortable there and graduated first in my class, it was an existence that did not necessarily prepare me for what was to come.

Thanks to my parents, however, I spent my summers away from McCormick and often had the opportunity to meet and interact with a more diverse group of children. After graduating from high school I entered Furman University, a place I had come to love from spending many summers there. Again, I was back in the role of being one of very few black students just as I had been in 4th grade. Little did I know at the time, I actually was creating a foundation that would prepare me for working in ANY environment. What comes with that is an ability to be comfortable dealing with the unknown and having to demonstrate value, credibility and worthiness sometimes when those around you think otherwise.

It requires developing a thick skin and an ability to endure sometimes when all odds are against you. It also makes you deal with the reality that some people out there are hoping you would fail. This reality helped me to be prepared and persevere even when the support was not there.

Whereas I felt very much supported through my time at Furman University, my sister had a totally different experience there. I was destined to major in psychology and worked with a group of professors who were encouraging and supportive. She, unfortunately, as a chemistry major, was perceived to be not "good enough" to pursue a career in medicine and was actually chided by her pre-medical advisor that she could not possibly land an acceptance to prestigious Harvard University. She received a letter of acceptance to Harvard and took it to this professor, who then proceeded to make disparaging comments as if it must have been some special program

Harvard had started for "black students." She clearly was accepted to Harvard based on the merits of her academic record, which was stellar, but this chemistry professor could not imagine that this little black girl from McCormick, South Carolina, had actually landed such an opportunity. Of course, she went on to Harvard, graduated with her M.D. degree, and today practices medicine in Atlanta.

I'm blessed to have had a totally opposite experience with psychology professors at Furman, who were my greatest cheerleaders. They were just as excited as my family when I landed my acceptance to the Ph.D. program at Emory University. Incidentally, in the late '70s and early '80s, I never had a faculty member of color at Furman University. And I was one of approximately 80 African American students attending Furman at the time. The total student enrollment was about 2,500. We were a close-knit group, and I now have lifelong friendships from my time there. You would not be surprised to know, however, that this close-knit group of friends was all African American. Again, a culture of separate but equal continued. We stuck together and did not venture much out of our comfort zone, not so much because we were not welcomed, but because it was just safer and more comfortable staying separate. I now have some regrets for not venturing outside of my comfort zone during my college years. You learn how to be a chameleon, being versatile enough to live in both worlds. Perhaps even learning a different language, one that was accepted in the classroom where you were often the only minority, and another in our own segregated environments, created by us.

I learned how to manage both worlds and brought with me my lessons learned from home and McCormick: to strive for excellence in all that you do; and achieve at a level much higher than anyone's expectation. That was my charge, and I set out to do just that.

PSYCHOLOGY AS THE FOUNDATION AND THE PATHWAY

I graduated from high school in three years and matriculated at Furman University in Greenville, South Carolina, with a desire to pursue a degree in education. Working with special needs children was my early passion, with my often wanting to find a way to help them achieve and accept their differences, and then encourage them to strive for success.

Along the way, however, I realized that being in the classroom was not necessarily my calling. I often grew impatient observing in the classroom. I was more curious about how to address the problem of these children head-on as opposed to trying to figure out how to teach them the basics of reading and math, sometimes when they clearly were preoccupied with other life challenges. Trying to teach when that child is hungry, distracted, mentally or physically abused, or overly excited just did not seem to be productive in my assessment of some of my early practical experiences in the classroom. Instead, my focus shifted. I evolved to a place where psychology became a passion, with a desire to figure out how the mind works and how our own psyche can influence the choices we make in life. The social circumstances and family dynamics that impacted the behavior of those children became more of a preoccupation and a vision for my career path.

So I changed my major from education to psychology and decided I would pursue an advanced degree and become a psychologist. After four engaging years at Furman, I graduated and entered Emory University to pursue a doctorate in clinical psychology. My career path seemed clear at that time, although I could not yet imagine all the many life lessons that would shape the way forward.

Becoming a psychologist was the initial career aspiration, and it became the foundation for all the many life lessons to be learned along the way. In particular, skill development in conflict resolution, listening, nonverbal communications, and interpersonal dynamics in leadership became quite useful along the way.

Those years at Emory University were challenging but equally fulfilling. There was a rigorous curriculum but I had comfort in knowing that what I was pursuing would add value and allow me to do fulfilling work. Completing my Ph.D. four years later was an awesome accomplishment, and I actually felt as if my world was finally opening up. I could be called "doctor," yet frankly, I felt completely inept and unprepared as I neared the end of my training. It is amazing how exhilarating the feeling of being conferred a doctorate degree is; accompanied by a sense of inadequacy and ineptness. Exhilaration and fear all at the same time! There was the impending panic of the question of "now what?" and "how do I start doing what I'm supposed to be doing?"

Of course, my dream was to be a psychologist. In my mind, that meant people would come to see me, share their deepest, darkest secrets, pay me, and then I would help them to resolve all their many issues. Essentially, I would fix what ailed them. Boy, was there now a rude awakening… the panic set in… I did not know where to start…. And, frankly, who in their right mind would come to see me (this still wet-behind the ears psychologist) to solve their problems? I had feelings of inadequacy, ineptness and the reality of not knowing where to start. So how do you build a practice of psychology fresh out of graduate school? With no track record? Just a fantastic degree from a great university, with a wonderful skill-set and book knowledge, but not yet credible.

By the time I graduated from Emory University with my Ph.D., I was a 25- year- old married woman with a toddler. I was married to Thaddeus Wadsworth Franklin, Jr. at the end of my first year of graduate school, and we welcomed our first son, Wesley Wadsworth Franklin, before I graduated. Shortly thereafter, I began a year-long clinical internship at Grady Memorial Hospital in Atlanta, working with seriously mentally ill patients. Personally, I hit another road block. I began to question my career path again. I had the degree in clinical psychology. I was interning at a major county hospital working with an indigent population, the neediest of the needy. I was struggling with whether I could be effective in treating this population. And, frankly, I questioned whether this was really what being a psychologist was all about.

Thaddeus and I struggled in those early years to make ends meet. We were both students with dreams for the future. We had love and determination to take us through those rough years, and we often look back and laugh at our innovative ways of surviving. My graduate stipend only went so far, but Thad worked several jobs including his own grass-cutting business to keep us going. Luckily, we had supportive family members who always made sure we did not sink too far.

My husband and I have always been supportive of each other's dream. Mine was to become a psychologist, and his was to one day own his own business. Along the way, life happens, however, and the dreams evolve. We managed to remember to love in spite of the road blocks and challenges along the way. And there were several.

We prayed through the struggles, and doors of opportunity were opened to us. Whereas I had begun to question my purpose and direction as I was completing my year-long internship at Grady, it was an opportunity I did not see coming that set a path for my career that I never imagined.

My degree in psychology opened the door for me to join the faculty of Morehouse School of Medicine. It was an opportunity that presented itself at a time that I never imagined teaching, especially not at a college level.

A MEDICAL SCHOOL...WHO KNEW?

I began applying for positions in my last few months of my year at Grady Memorial Hospital. I actually considered a few entry level therapist/counselor positions. However, as fate would have it, I was approached about joining the faculty of Morehouse School of Medicine (MSM) as a faculty member, teaching medical students. MSM was a relatively new, small, free-standing medical school founded in 1975 at the Historically Black Morehouse College. The year was 1986 and it had just graduated its second class of MD students. In the shadows of Emory University, this second medical school in town was developed through the shear will and determination of Dr. Louis W. Sullivan. Dr. Sullivan was the founding dean and first president of Morehouse School of Medicine. When I arrived in 1986 I began teaching first- and second- year medical students a course in behavioral sciences and psychopathology. Whereas I had initially considered education (i.e., special education) as a major in college, I had given up on the idea of being a teacher as I changed my undergraduate major from education to psychology. Joining a medical school faculty was intriguing, and I accepted the challenge to become an assistant professor at this relatively new medical school, fresh out of graduate school. Little did I know at the time, saying "yes" to MSM would be the foundation that would define my entire career trajectory.

I accepted the challenge and joined the faculty. Teaching became a passion, and I was surprised at how much I really enjoyed it, being a psychologist and a teacher all at once. Those early years at MSM were great. I learned how to navigate the classroom, prepare lectures and engage professional students in learning. Being at a small, developing institution, I also had the opportunity to engage administratively, serving on committees, leading task forces and writing reports, which allowed me to grow and expand in a way that my colleagues in much larger institutions would never have been allowed to do. I became the "mickey" on campus, the "go to" person, and I considered myself a "sponge," eager to learn and soak it all in.

The most important life lesson, however, came to me a few years after being at Morehouse School of Medicine. While I had been trying to "order my own steps" and decide what I WOULD become, I realized that I really did not have the control that I thought I had. I was busy being a wife and mother and medical school faculty member as my husband was developing a career path as an administrator in finance at Emory University. We were able to handle our bills, save a little for a rainy day, and actually plan an occasional vacation. Life was good! But I still was not sure where all this would take me. I planned to stay at Morehouse School of Medicine for five years, just long enough to build a clinical practice. I was able to build my practice through the faculty practice plan and got referrals from the other physicians in the clinic. I also tested the waters in building scholarly pursuits by accepting a fellowship with the National Institute on Drug Abuse through its research training and career development for young investigators program. This all seemed to be moving fast, and a career path was being shaped for me with very little direction of my own. I decided I needed to just accept things as they were and go with the flow.

I let go. This now became more of a spiritual journey, realizing that sometimes life will provide you a roller coaster ride that you never intended to get on.

Within a few years of my arrival at MSM, I was presented with other opportunities that expanded my role. I became director of counseling services first, then eventually was appointed to the dean's staff as an assistant dean for admissions. I thoroughly enjoyed each new opportunity and saw them as quite an adventure. I surprised myself at how much I was able to grow and learn in each role.

As a family, we were also growing as we welcomed Grant Alexander Franklin in 1990 and Jordan Walker Franklin in 1994. My husband, Thaddeus, completed his master's degree in health care administration along the way and moved from finance into clinic and hospital administration. We were busy with the boys and all their many activities as we maintained a very good and progressive family life.

I had planned to stay at MSM for five years, which became 10 years, which became 15 years. I began questioning whether or not I was staying in the same place much too long. I enjoyed my job, and it was a fulfilling career given the direct impact I would have in nurturing and supporting the careers of the future physicians being trained at MSM. I cannot pinpoint the exact date, but in the late '90s I grew weary. I was about to cross the 15-year mark and I really did not know where I was going. I remember telling my kids that I had begun to question what I really wanted to do and that frankly I did not know what I wanted to be when I "grew up." Of course, as kids, they thought this was quite strange to hear from their mother. I was doing a job, and relatively successful at it. I was making my mark at MSM, and the students really seemed to appreciate it. But had I lost myself in the shuffle?

FINDING PURPOSE

As I progressed through my career, I became more aware of my own personal strength and conviction. As my faith grew, I began to see my purpose as something much more than just following a career path.

I was honored to be selected to join the Board of Trustees of my alma mater, Furman University, in 1999, and I was extremely excited to attend my first board meeting. It was in my first board meeting that I met the now deceased George Keller, a nationally known expert in higher education and strategic planning. Dr. Keller was selected to facilitate a board retreat at Furman on diversity. As the only person of color in the room at my first board retreat, I was quite amused to hear him talk about the changing demographic and what Furman University must do to prepare for a more diverse and inclusive student body. As a member of the student body when the magic number was 80 students of color, I found it refreshing to hear Dr. Keller challenge the board and its leadership. He seemed equally intrigued with my presence and this began a relationship that I came to treasure. It was actually Dr. Keller who first suggested to me that I "step out of my comfort zone" and reach.

He explained that he thought I had stayed too long at Morehouse School of Medicine (MSM) and I was destined for something greater. He encouraged me to consider the American Council on Education

Fellows Program, which was designed to prepare the next generation of leaders in higher education. I remember saying to him that such an opportunity could never happen for me given I was coming from such a small institution with very meager resources. With his insistence I approached the President of Morehouse School of Medicine, Dr. Louis W. Sullivan, who by then had been to Washington, DC, as Secretary of the Department of Health and Human Services under President George W. Bush. After four years, he had returned as president again of MSM. He had always been very supportive and someone I still consider a mentor. But to ask him to support me in the ACE Fellows Program meant a financial investment in my future with a requirement that I continue to receive my full-time salary although I would be away for the full year assigned to work with another mentor in another institution. With Louis Sullivan's endorsement and George Keller's letter of support, I applied for the ACE Fellows program and was selected as one of 43 higher education administrators to participate in the 2001-02 academic year. To aid in making sure my job at MSM was managed I stayed in Atlanta and selected Oglethorpe University, a small liberal arts school, and its then-president, Dr. Larry Large, for my fellowship assignment. I began in the fall of 2001 and my spiritual journey kicked into overdrive.

I considered the year as an ACE Fellow at Oglethorpe with Dr. Large my year of affirmation. I enjoyed the opportunity to learn from a president who allowed me to shadow him throughout the day. We often talked of the leadership challenges he faced and his support and encouragement helped to shape my perspective on the commitment college presidents must make. During this time, I realized that my purpose was a calling to a college presidency. It seemed impossible at that point and I did not know how, when or where, but I stepped out on faith and as one of my spiritual advisors once told me: *Be still, listen, let go, Let GOD!*

I must admit, along the way I was challenged, tested, and almost broken but I persevered. I was struggling for purpose and seemed to find it or perhaps it found me.

Over my 20 years at MSM, this roller coaster ride; or the train ride that I sometimes called it, allowed me to advance in a way that I never imagined. Simply working hard, doing the right thing and asking for help along the way.

I decided I would latch on to the coat tails of those who were in the seats that I admired. I also took advantage of as many opportunities as possible to provide and grow in leadership. I looked to others for leadership and mentorship and I was never denied. Simply asking for advice, engaging with others and showing a genuine eagerness to learn became the trademarks of my existence. I learned a lot, I gave a lot, yet, over time I became impatient and weary with the next step.

I also struggled for validation and I faced self-doubt along the way. It was exhilarating and enlightening to go through my year of training as an ACE fellow, but I felt "stuck" with no sense of a way to get out. My year of affirmation was a roller coaster ride of emotions. I was pleased that I was able to keep all the balls in the air as I juggled my many responsibilities at MSM, Oglethorpe and the ACE Fellows Program while maintaining my household and family. However, I did not know where I would go from there. I was expected to return to MSM for at least one year to bring something back to advance the organization that sponsored and invested in me. I learned about strategic planning while away and came back to MSM a year later to launch its first comprehensive strategic planning process. Things were different, however….. or perhaps I was different. My mentor, Dr. Louis W. Sullivan, had announced his retirement and the school had a new president, but I also had a new attitude about my future. I no longer felt compelled to stay, and it was time to go test my wings. Breaking out of my comfort zone was now much easier. I just needed to pay my dues, then move forward.

As mentioned earlier, the year as an ACE Fellow was my year of affirmation...the year I knew my purpose... that I would aspire to be a college president. I did not know how I would get there, but I knew that was my calling.

Not only did I give MSM the expected year, but it was actually five more years before I would leave. It was five years of self-doubt and frustration as I constantly struggled with finding my way out. The work remained fulfilling simply because of my love for the job and the students I was serving. It was frustrating, however, because I was hoping for more and there was a feeling of being stuck. I continued to pray to ask for guidance and patience as my faith grew.

The opportunity to go to Meharry Medical College in 2007 as an executive vice president and provost was an unexpected part of the journey. Again, it meant I was advancing in the right direction but still not sure when or where I would end up. I was hopeful but fearful at the same time. Actually, my greatest challenge came during my time at Meharry Medical College. For the first time, my efforts were questioned and not appreciated. It was a tough environment culturally, and I was perceived to be an outsider. I had planned to stay no more than three years but at the end of year one, I realized I would be tested in a way that I had never imagined. Regardless, I needed to do my job with the same level of integrity and fortitude and with the same spirit of camaraderie and mutual respect, even when it was not reciprocated.

So, I pressed on..... doing what I was called to do.....forever being in the moment....forever trying to do the right thing....maintaining integrity..... being respectful of others.... And remembering the Golden Rule; treating others as I would have wanted to be treated. The small-town values remained!

THE UNLIKELY CHOICE

By the end of my second year at Meharry, it was clear that I needed to start moving forward. The role was challenging, yet, I had agreed to stay for three years and I knew it would likely take a year to search for my next job. I never lost sight of my calling, and this, too, was a part of my spiritual journey. I accepted it as it was, and realized that the struggles there were simply part of the journey. I reached out to my many mentors to begin the conversation of next steps. I was given considerable latitude in my role at Meharry thanks to then-president, Dr. Wayne J. Riley. Serving as the chief operations officer/executive vice president as well as the chief academic officer/provost allowed me to grow my portfolio of work with expanded opportunities to provide leadership at another health sciences university. At the same time, I knew I could not stay much longer than three years. I frankly thought I was in the wrong type of university. As a Ph.D., I assumed I was a better fit in a more traditional comprehensive college or university. I assumed that if I continued to aspire to become a college president, my chances would be limited the longer I stayed in a health sciences university...or so I thought!

With the help of several mentors, I quickly began being nominated for college presidencies from small liberal arts colleges to more traditional comprehensive universities. Each time I submitted an application, I would say a prayer and ask for guidance in the interview. Over the next year, I had several chances to do the "airport interview" and actually moved to the final three in two searches for president. This renewed my spirit and I began regaining a sense of hope.

I had considerable doubt in my ability to compete for a college presidency. The arduous search process had taken a toll, and whereas I was having increasing success in progressing through the process, I often had the feeling of "probably not me!"

After the second failed search, I began to consider myself the unlikely choice for a president. I had type-cast myself in the health sciences, which did not translate well in searches for liberal arts colleges. I had tried to remain in the South initially because of family ties, but it became obvious that many traditional colleges and universities in the South were not yet ready for a person of color. So I remained vigilant yet cautious in my search.

The call from a search consultant in the summer of 2010 was a surprise. I had just withdrawn from a search for personal reasons, and it was coincidental that the firm handling that search was also handling the search for the next president of Des Moines University (DMU).

In my early conversations with the search consultant, I gave him several reasons why it was "not me." First, this was a health sciences university, and in my previous experiences I could have only imagined a physician in the top seat. I questioned the desire of the board to hire a physician and was told repeatedly that this was an open search and the board was eager to interview and consider a diverse group of candidates. And frankly, I was told, the previous president was a former state governor. You can imagine my reaction to that.

My second thought of being the unlikely candidate was the fact that if the DMU board members did not want a physician and had once had the governor, they clearly were likely to hire another politician. So, again, not me! And the scenario goes back to my own self-doubt about being female and a woman of color. I had experienced quizzical looks from campus constituents and search committee members in other searches (primarily in the South) who seemed to question whether they were ready for an African American woman as president. I doubted they were ready and thought it likely was NOT ME because I assumed it would not be a good fit.

So when the phone call came from DMU, there were several reasons why I believed I was the unlikely candidate: non- physician, non-politician, non-male, non-caucasian. I failed to acknowledge the obvious: my self-doubt was getting in the way. The script of "probably not me" colored my impressions. And whereas I was well prepared for higher education administration, having provided leadership covering mostly every aspect of academe, I failed to give myself credit. Unfortunately, the self-talk, the self-doubt, the negative script of "probably not me" was being replayed over and over in my mind. The self-talk was winning. It was a sense that many women have of being all things for everyone else, but sometimes not giving ourselves credit for all the great accomplishments we have achieved. Actually, most women administrators typically feel they have to check all the boxes, often being more comprehensive in their preparation, training and experiences than some male counterparts who are competing for college presidencies.

Little did I know, many members of the DMU Board and its search committee were thinking it COULD BE ME, and simply wondered whether I would accept if offered. I now enjoy hearing the stories from my current chair of the Board, Dr. Larry Baker, and immediate-pass Chair, Dr. James Grekin, who share stories of considerable excitement about the prospects of my leadership at DMU. So, whereas I thought I was the unlikely choice, it seemed that I was the only one thinking so. Amazing how we can be so wrong in our impressions. Amazing how we can be our own worst enemy.

The mere fact that it was a phone call from a search firm one day, and not my seeking this opportunity, has validated for me that I am not at Des Moines University because of my own choosing, but due to truly divine intervention. I have come to acknowledge the fact that my steps had been ordered by a power much greater than I. No one could have ever predicted that I would be in Iowa. So I let go and let God...and here I am today.

The calling to the presidency was to come to Iowa, to Des Moines University, to make an impact on the lives of those who are called to serve, future health care providers. It has been an unconventional journey with several twists and turns, and I was perceived to be an unlikely choice. Then again, I was wrong!

LESSONS LEARNED

I am honored to serve as the 15th president of Des Moines University. I am entering my fourth year and I am thrilled to be in a position to make history as the first woman and person of color to serve this 115-year- old institution. Prior to my arrival, I had already begun shaping thoughts on leadership and institutional effectiveness. Frankly, I have learned most by noting the things I would NOT do if I were to ever become a president. Many of my thoughts on leadership stem from some core principles and values that have roots in my childhood. The lessons learned as a little small town girl in McCormick, South Carolina, have stayed with me and laid the foundation for how I treat people and work collaboratively with all.

As a young child, I was always the one helping everyone else. From tutoring my classmates in elementary school, just because I wanted everyone to understand, to being the sounding board for many of my friends through high school and college, I often gave advice and perspective when others needed help.

As a young faculty member and later as an administrator, I often became the "go to" person as others looked to me to be very direct, thoughtful and respectful in my assessment of issues and challenges we faced on campus. The analogy I use most to describe myself is that I have a knack of being able to see the forest AND each distinct tree. I could envision where each tree was planted, and I even knew how to clear the brush. I could communicate that to others in a non-threatening manner, which I came to realize was respected and appreciated by others. I was often asked what we needed to do and how to get everyone to work collaboratively to get us there.

It was natural for me to have chosen psychology as a major. I was intrigued with how the mind worked and how our own self-talk could be used to encourage or detract from making progress. I am a firm believer in the power of the mind and the synergistic relationship between mind, body and soul. I allowed my own negative and doubtful self-talk to color my sense of worthiness and validation. The recognition of this allowed me to focus more on what is most important- faith and contentment.

Being true to self and being authentic are where I begin and encourage others to do so. To live a lie cheats everyone but most importantly leads others to question, doubt and wonder what is real.

My philosophy of leadership takes into consideration my own personal dynamics in terms of how I see people and treat people. The approach that comes closest to my philosophy is servant leadership. The phrase "servant leadership" was coined by Robert K. Greenleaf in *The Servant as Leader*, an essay that he first published in 1970. In that essay, he said:

"The servant-leader *is* servant first... It begins with the natural feeling that one wants to serve, to serve *first*. Then conscious choice brings one to aspire to lead. That person is sharply different from one who is *leader* first. The difference manifests itself in the care taken by the servant-first to make sure that other people's highest priority needs are being served."

From this philosophy, I have come to embrace as one of my favorite quotes from William Arthur Ward's manuscript on "Leadership.... with a human touch" the following:

We must be silent before we can listen. We must listen before we can learn. We must learn before we can prepare. We must prepare before we can serve. We must serve before we can lead.

For me, servant leadership is just a fancy way to talk about applying the Golden Rule to leadership- treating people with respect, in a manner in which I would expect to be treated, and with a desire to be of service as opposed to being served.

Along the way, in my unconventional journey, I have learned several lessons that are described below. Perhaps they could even be described as necessary qualities for successful leadership. I do not profess to have it all covered or yet all learned. As I continue to travel along my personal journey, I'm sure this list will grow and expand. For life itself is an evolution.

LEADERSHIP QUALITIES

ONE: Have the right attitude

There is nothing more important than one's outlook and personal style. I believe effective leaders need to begin with a correct mind-set, which includes a genuine desire and willingness to serve others. It is a conscious decision to step up in the role, amid challenges with a clear focus. Without the right mind-set, a leader will not be able to ensure that group goals are met. Instead, there will be an appearance that actions are being taken for personal gain. The worst mistake a leader can make is taking on the role with the attitude that they have arrived and it is all about them.

The theory of servant leadership is the backdrop for my style of leadership, which begins with first having the right attitude. It is never about the individual but about the organization. The more positive, "glass-half-full" attitude the leader has, then the more likely it will become contagious and spreading.

TWO: Mutual Respect

An essential ingredient in leadership is a genuine desire to value people as people and to treat them the way you would want to be treated. There have been some very interesting twists on this statement which raises a question about whether or not someone can know someone well enough to know exactly how they want to be treated. So, believe it or not, there has been a "challenge" to the Golden Rule. What is fascinating about this is that those who choose to raise this question seem to be forgetting a basic principle, which is simply mutual respect. Who would NOT want to be treated with kindness and respect? Plain and simple, we should all value this basic principle. I do not need to know much more about the person other than the fact that he or she is human and deserves such respect.

On the other hand, there may be value in acknowledging that we are all different coming from different cultures and experiences, and it is important to reach people where they are. But I would say it is likely impossible to really KNOW everyone well enough to know exactly how they want to be treated. The basic premise of the Golden Rule focuses on the basics of respect, compassion and kindness. It does not matter if I know your culture or ethnicity. There simply is a universal standard of treating people with kindness. We all can do that regardless of who we are and where we come from.

THREE: Listen

Psychologists are trained to be good listeners. There is a skill involved, but it is also a very simple thing to do. Communication is a two-way process, and it is so important for a leader to learn how to sometimes shut up and listen. Stephen Covey says: "Seek first to understand, then seek to be understood." This reflects the epitome of effective listening. Everyone is entitled to his or her own opinion, and it is so important to value the opinions of all. There is the phrase often used that states that you should allow everyone to have "voice," which simply means it is important to give everyone an opportunity to be heard. Ineffective listening undermines one's self-esteem, self-confidence and creativity. Think of the impact of empowering someone who has a great idea to feel as if their opinion is actually valued and heard. It also is most important to acknowledge that hearing and listening are not synonymous. The worst mistake a leader can make is sitting quietly to hear someone speak, then in the very next breath, run over them with your own "better idea" without acknowledging that you heard or valued anything that was said.

FOUR: Honesty and truthfulness

I pride myself on being an authentic person, flaunting no frills, being consistent and calling it as I see it. Being trustworthy is an essential ingredient to maintaining credibility in a leadership role. Your word is everything and, believe me, there are so many times that your words are misconstrued or misinterpreted that it is so important that you are genuine and consistent. I find myself having to correct misrepresentations of things that I say. If I am honest and consistent in my message, then it is easy to clean up misinterpretations. However, if my story keeps changing and I represent different messages depending on the circumstances, then it is more difficult to clear misinterpretations. Being authentic allows me to be real, genuine and consistent.

As for honesty and truthfulness, your word is your word. It is entirely possible to be truthful and compassionate all at the same time. It is never right, however, to malign someone and make hurtful statements. We gain nothing from being brutally honest when we mean only to hurt. Yet beginning with honesty allows one to be perceived to be trustworthy.

FIVE: Expect conflict

I wish the world were a perfect place to be! I can wish all people would be perfect, but we are not. We are all flawed with our own little quirks. And the richness of the interactions with others comes from the diversity of opinion that we all bring to the table. We are bound to have differing opinions, which leads to conflict. I expect it and plan for it. In any work or family situation, conflict is inevitable and a constant factor in human interactions. An effective leader expects conflict and is able to manage it in a productive manner. It is never easy to manage conflict, but leaders must make a concerted effort to set expectations and build a culture of openness. When conflicts arrive, it is important to get the issues on the table for all to see and deal with the issues in a timely manner, because prolonging that only makes matters worse.

This is the most difficult of the qualities to manage because of the emotionality of conflict. Many times conflicts occur because people are not able to differentiate between task-related conflict issues and their personal investment in a given situation. It is so important to separate the two. When conflicts get personalized it is more difficult to separate feelings from facts. The facts can be more easily addressed if the feelings are acknowledged and put into proper perspective. Do I expect to get along with everyone all the time? Do I expect to have everyone be pleased and happy with decisions that are made? No! The feelings of happiness, satisfaction, pleasure and contentment should be by-products of the good will that comes from working together to manage conflict in a civil, collegial manner, staying focused on the facts and the need for finding common ground and resolution.

SIX: Be proactive

Early in my tenure as a faculty member, I was often in the position of either volunteering to serve on committees or lead a particular work group or project. I was always eager to learn and looked at every new opportunity as resume building. Knowledge is power and the more you engage the more you learn. Stepping up to the plate to lead allowed me to become validated. Inserting yourself into the mix gives you visibility and credibility. When all else fails, ask for the opportunity!

This is very similar to the impressions shared in Sheryl Sandberg's book, *Lean In*. Too many times women in particular sit on their hands and wait for someone else to take the lead. I remember once being told that I should not always volunteer to take the minutes in meetings since it was perceived to be expected of the women in the group. I often found myself being the only female in several meetings early on in my career. I did not mind taking the minutes and recording what happened in meetings and never thought of it as demeaning or stereotypical. What it gave me, eventually, was an opportunity to lead. For she who takes the minutes controls the history! As the recorder of the action steps, I soon became the go-to person who knew how to set the next agenda because I had the details from the previous meeting. Being proactive and stepping up to the plate can be empowering and impactful. Don't underestimate the power of the small step!

SEVEN: Commitment

As I struggled with purpose along my journey, I found myself questioning my level of commitment. I often asked why I was still at Morehouse School of Medicine after 20 years. Clearly, I was committed to the mission of the school but even more so to the students I served. I often joked with the students that I made a personal commitment to them in helping them to achieve their goal as I called their names out to introduce them at first-year orientation. Somehow, my commitment extended to seeing them cross the stage at graduation as I was able to be the first to call them "doctor" as they were conferred their degrees. That commitment to the students perhaps was why I stayed there so long. My engagement was that as soon as I brought a new class of students in, I felt a commitment to seeing them march across the stage.

It was a difficult shift in my thinking about commitment that allowed me to let go of that very restricted and limiting approach. Yes, I maintained my commitment to aid and assist future health professionals in reaching their goal, but I realized I did not necessarily have to do so only at this one institution.

That commitment, however, was what kept me going during the challenging times. I was in it for all the right reasons, and getting caught up in the mission of the school was easy. It was not about me, and it was not just giving lip service. It is so important to exude commitment through thoughts and actions. Ask yourself: are you really in it for the right reasons?

EIGHT: Take risks

One trait of a great leader is an ability to take risks. If you are risk-adverse, beware. It is so important to be able to step outside of the box and to think innovatively. Flexibility of thought and action is a must. A leader must also be able to know when it's time to try a new approach or implement a new policy. Being stuck in a rut with comfort as the status quo never advances an agenda. Be a student of your own profession. Learn, be innovative, do your homework and get a grasp on what the best practices are. No one wants a stagnant, status quo leader. There is excitement in innovation that pushes your organization forward.

NINE: Acknowledge authority and adhere to policies

Everyone has a boss and everyone has to answer to someone. I, first, answer to a spiritual power and I get my faith from this most exalted leader. However, it is equally important to show respect and be accountable to those in authority even when you do not believe they have earned your respect. Your boss is your boss until you choose to be somewhere else. In the same vein, it is important to adhere to the policies of the organization, staying aligned with the organization's goals and procedures until it is perceived that there is a need for change. There are some environments where written policies, which were established in the past, are ignored as everyone chooses to instead follow the "practice" and guidelines that have evolved over time. As the leader, you, therefore, have demonstrated that there are NO policies. A leader should acknowledge when there is a need to create policy where there are none existing, change policies that no longer work, and abide by those that exist. Otherwise, the integrity of processes becomes undermined.

TEN: Team spirit

It is so important to build trust within an organization. This is another one of those principles that takes quite a bit of time to achieve. It is important to set clear expectations and let people do their jobs. It is also important to create an environment where people matter and to foster a sense of team spirit and camaraderie. I love the idea of the "warm fuzzy" and a simple acknowledgement of thanks is so easy to do. People want to feel that they are valued members of a team. A simple gesture of saying "thank you for all that you do" goes a long way in building morale and fostering a sense of team spirit.

ELEVEN: Take things lightly

The phrase "don't sweat the small stuff" is used to express a desire for not getting bogged down in minutiae. There are conflicts and challenges in any work environment, but it is so important to focus on what is most important, decide whether the battle is worth fighting and remain cool, calm and collected. There will be days when you feel like nothing worked and everything is broken. I sometimes talk of the fires that are blazing all around me some days and I cannot seem to get anything done. There is always the unexpected situation that appears out of nowhere. I believe by nature I typically do not let myself get too excited, and I choose to not wear my feelings on my sleeve. This is a skill that can be taught if it is not instinctive. The best sign of leadership during challenging times is one who can calmly focus, think clearly and strategically, and directly address the issue. Keeping emotions at bay is also important. One should learn to take things likely, do not sweat the small stuff and create a mental "parking lot" to hold things that you cannot understand or explain and leave it there. Then "go home" ready to fight another day. There is no perfect environment and no perfect people. The institutions we serve will still have challenges when we leave, and we will never be able to make them perfect. Striving for perfection is fine, but more important is knowing how to celebrate the small successes that help to move an organization forward.

TWELVE: Take care of yourself

My training in psychology has allowed me to remain focused on ensuring that I maintain my own sanity in a sometimes-insane world. I am a major proponent of prevention and wellness, and to work in an institution with wellness as a core value is an ever greater testament of me being in the right place. We all know the basic rules of living a healthy lifestyle, but many still struggle on how to do the right thing. I believe there are psychological and personality variables that help to define who can be successful in a disciplined approach to health and wellness. Eat right, exercise, do what the doctor says seems simple enough, but we often do not take our own advice. It is important to reduce the stress level in our lives as best we can but, even more importantly, recognize when things are out of control and when you need help. It is so important to seek help early. Taking good care of yourself and being a bit selfish when it comes to that allows you to be available and ready to help others.

The serenity prayer sums it up nicely:

"God grant me the serenity to accept the things I cannot change, courage to change the things I can and wisdom to know the difference."

CLOSING

The above twelve principles of leadership have allowed me to move forward in my career. I take them all to heart and try to remind myself daily if I am applying these principles. When I set out on this journey, I did not know I would be where I am today. I remained open to all possibilities. I rode the train of opportunity and allowed it to take me places I never dreamed. I am where I am supposed to be at this particular point in time, because as I have heard reflected from ministers in the pulpit, "what is for me is for me!" I do not try to determine anymore what I am supposed to do. I allow my faith to carry me forward. I will grow where I am planted, then bloom as much as I can. I am comfortable in my own skin and remain true to myself. I have re-written the script of self-doubt and no longer allow the negative self-talk to interfere. I have evolved to this place and the journey is not yet over. This was a dream fulfilled but work is still yet to be done! I will continue to DREAM BIG! Not just because it sounds good, but because it is a personal imperative!

Perhaps it was an unconventional journey, but it was MINE! You, too, are on your own journey, and, perhaps divine intervention will take you to places you have never imagined. Perhaps you, too, are an unlikely choice. Or so you may think.

REFERENCES/CITATIONS

Bible, New Revised Standard Version, Division of Christian Education of the National Council of the Churches of Christ in the United States of America, 1989.

Brown v Board of Education of Topeka. Opinion: May 17, 1954. Records of the Supreme Court of the United States, Record Group 267, National Archives.

Covey, Stephen. *7 Habits of Highly Effective People*, 1989.

Greenleaf, Robert K. *Servant Leadership – A journey into the Nature of Legitimate Power and Greatness,* Paulist Press, 1977.

Niebuhr, Reinhold. The Serenity Prayer, 1943.

Sandberg, Sheryl. *Lean In: Women, Work and the Will to Lead,* 2013.

Ward, William Arthur. *Leadership....With a Human Touch,* June 1, 1999.

CPSIA information can be obtained
at www.ICGtesting.com
Printed in the USA
LVHW040932060520
655001LV00002B/404